Made to Have
DOMINION

Why God Created Us

FIRST EDITION

 KENNETH J. COLEMAN

Made to Have

DOMINION

Why God Created Us

All quotations from Scripture are taken from the
New Scofield Study Bible, Authorized King James
Version, 2002

HigherLife Publishing & Marketing
PO Box 623307
Oviedo, FL 32762
AHigherLife.com

Made to Have Dominion/Kenneth J. Coleman –
1st ed.

ISBN 978-1-951492-65-6 Paperback
ISBN 978-1-951492-51-9 eBook
ISBN 978-1-951492-72-4 Audiobook

10 9 8 7 6 5 4 3 2 1
Printed in the United States of America.

This book is one of the greatest well-organized piece of literature dealing with God's kingdom reigning on the earth. It's a simplistic profound revelation of the power, order and peace that God gave His people to conquer all opposition. We, as Christians are equipped with a heavenly battle plan to expand God's kingdom.

—Pastor Clarence Williams

One of the best, if not the BEST book I've ever read! Once you start reading it, you will not put it down. In this book you will find your purpose and identity in life. EVERY believer should add this book to their biblical collection. It's a great tool I've used to teach and preach from because it's VERY inspiring and edifying. The book is VERY sound. It's not religious, it's SPIRITUAL. The book is about the Kingdom of GOD. I have been in ministry for 30 plus years and it's not every day we find written in a book, how to LIVE and act accordingly with the authority that God gave us as Christians. I urge you, don't pass up this opportunity to better your everyday walk with the LORD. You won't regret getting this book. You can and will walk with your heads lifted up, operating in Kingdom principles for the rest of your life.

I promise you will ENJOY every chapter of this book.

—Pastor J. L. Daniels III,
Founder of God Did It Outreach Ministries in
Haughton, La...Blessings

What I got from the book *Made to Have Dominion* is very important to me. I think it will help other kids and adults realize who they are. What I like about this book is that it's not very sugar coated, it tells the truth and what it says, that's what it means. I recommend this book to anybody else who's looking to find salvation and themselves. I learned from this book to not lean on my own understanding. The way to heaven is Jesus. You have dominion over the earth and when I say the earth I mean everything; mountains, grass, trees, bushes, houses and even water. The way to find that dominion is to seek the Father and if you want to see the Father read the Bible and read this book. I hope this book helps you. God bless whoever reads this.

—Ashley Mark Prince, age 11

Reading *Made to Have Dominion* has opened my eyes to the amount of power I have over my life and the world around me. The Lord graciously gave me dominion over this world and because of this new revelation I have drawn closer to him so that my will can be his will.

—Sabrai Mark, age 16

I have been blessed and honored to read *Made to Have Dominion*. It has encouraged me to use the authority God has given me. This book has changed my life for the better, making me realize the important role I play in the Kingdom of God. He has commanded me to have dominion over the earth, and just that simple command has humbled me, causing me to realize how much power God has given me, and what a honor it is. This book has truly been written through a vessel by God himself.

—Asia Roland, age 17

Dedication

This dedication is for the one person whom I admire the most, and that would be Tovonia Gossett Coleman, my wife. It is she to whom I give this greatest of honor. No one could be more well deserving. It has been her steadfastness, persistence, and resilience over these many years for the things of God that has allowed me to come to this place in life at this very moment. Because of her, everything that God has been doing in our lives is made complete. So a very special thanks to Tovonia for her love and what she has meant to me over the years.

Now unto the King eternal, immortal, invisible, the only wise God, the blessed and only Potentate, the King of kings, and the Lord of lords; be honor and glory forever and ever. Amen.

Acknowledgments

First and foremost I would like to acknowledge all who have helped to get this book finished with their prayers, giving, and various support. Such as the prayer group in Lubbock Texas, and also Kimberly Williams, who was the first to put this manuscript in reading form. To our daughters Shondolyn and Kendra whom we love and are very proud of. To Greg and Lenda Crawford, my pastors, for their support and belief in me. And to Cathy Cornett, who has always been a vital part of what we do. Finally to our daughter in Christ, Carla Willis, for working side by side with us in giving of her time, and expertise.

CONTENTS

Chapter 1

THIS WAY OF THINKING

Take the Challenge

Let's just imagine for a moment that God offered you absolute authority over all the earth for one month. You are in charge, whatever you say goes, your word is law. Would you take it? That will give you a lot of freedom to do whatever you want. But it also means that you would have an enormous responsibility for what will and will not happen on the earth. You won't be able to blame God for anything that goes wrong. You know that's what we do. We say things like, "Why doesn't God do something about all this evil and suffering in the world? How can a God of love allow sickness and disease and all these things to continue to happen? Why doesn't He do something to stop it?"

You know how wise God is. He never waits until we need something before He provides it. He puts the answer in the midst of us, or He puts it in us, or both. Every king has a kingdom, and in that kingdom he has dominion. Heaven is a kingdom, and in that Kingdom God has complete dominion. And God said, "Let us make man in our image, after our likeness, and let them have dominion…over all the earth, and over every creeping thing that creeps and moves upon the earth" (Gen 1:26). That is exactly what God did in the beginning when He created man; He gave him dominion over this earthly kingdom. We were made to be like Him, and to look like Him, which is to say, in our character, to act like Him, and to function like He functions. God is Spirit, so is man; He speaks words, so does man. He is a king, so is man. He operates in faith, so does man. He has dominion, He's in charge, He gives command, and so does man (woman)—that is, if they are citizens of His Kingdom. We were made to be like Him.

Who's Responsible?

Some would say, "But how can we be in charge when God is the one who is in control of everything on this earth?" Everything is under His authority, or subject to it. Realize this, if God was actually in control of everything that happens on this earth, then earth would be exactly as heaven is right now. Since He is not, then the responsibility falls completely on us.

Let us no longer focus on what God has or has

not allowed to happen on the earth, but instead let us focus on what we have or have not allowed to happen on this earth. Whether God allowed something to happen or not is not more important than the reality of what He has given us, and that is for us to have dominion over it.

God is sovereign, and yes, He can do anything that He chooses to do. And He has done exactly that. In and by His own sovereign will, He has chosen to give man dominion and control on the earth. Therefore, God's control on earth is limited because it comes through those whom He controls. I call that doing what you want to. He uses *us* to bring things under *His* control. No, I do not assume that I know all there is about the sovereignty of God, and surely there are things that happen in this world that we do not fully understand, but that does not excuse us from what He has said about *our* dominion authority. I do know this; we are in charge, therefore responsible for what happens here on earth. You and I have something to say about what happens on this planet.

A demonstration of dominion authority was displayed by a group of about 200 children in the country of Kenya. In February 2008, in a small tin shack of a Baptist Church, children started getting together on their own to pray against the post-election violence in their country, especially, in the hard-hit slums of Nairobi. The pastor told an overseas correspondent for the International Mission Board that ever since the children started praying together, there have been no deaths, houses burned, or even violence in their section of the slums. Even the adults recited this fact in amazement.

The children, however, didn't even mention it because it's exactly what they expected to happen. In Matt. 18:18 Jesus said, "I tell you the truth." My question is, why would Jesus, who is the truth, have to say to us, "I tell you the truth"? As if there was a need to qualify this particular statement as true. No! It is because what He was about to say was so unbelievably true that it totally escapes all human reasoning and imagination. Only the mind of a child can receive something like this. Jesus says, "Whatsoever you shall bind [not permit, not allow, not except, lock up, refuse, or prohibit] on earth, shall be bound in heaven, and whatsoever you, [the emphasis is on *you*] shall loose [permit, accept, allow, unlock, not refuse] on earth, shall be loosed in heaven" (Matt. 18:18). Remember, He has given us the keys of the Kingdom of heaven.

Use your dominion authority. Jesus said, "The knowledge of the secrets of the Kingdom of God has been given to you" (Matt. 13:10). In Luke 8:10 He also said, "Again I say unto you that if two of you shall agree on earth as touching anything [ANYTHING!!!]

that they shall ask, it shall be done for them by my Father who is in heaven" (Matt. 18:19).

The Lack of Responsibility

Man was created with a dominion mandate over the earth, giving him the responsibility to represent the Kingdom government of God on earth. Jesus said, "And I confer on you a kingdom just as my Father conferred one on Me" (Luke 22:29). The word "confer" means to appoint, to bestow, (giving honor) to designate, or to assign authority to a position or an office.

It is no one else's responsibility to govern in Heaven's earthly kingdom other than those who have been assigned authority to do so. In a Democratic Republic form of government, judges are appointed by the President, not elected, and so are the Cabinet members; they are also appointed. So in God's Kingdom government you and I have also been appointed by the King Himself, who is Christ. Seeking first the Kingdom of God and His righteousness is the key to all of this. I know this is going to cause you to have to change some things, but this is why Jesus said, "Repent, for the kingdom of Heaven is here" (Matt. 3:2). And the only thing you really have to change is the way you think, which is what "repent" means. It means to think differently, to change the way you're thinking because the way you think determines the way you live and believe.

Jesus knew that in order for anyone to access the power and authority of the Kingdom of heaven, they can't continue to think the way they have been thinking. The scripture says in Isaiah 55:8 that God's ways and thoughts are higher than ours. That does not mean that you can't have them. No! That means we need to allow Him to raise our level of thinking and our way of thinking up to His.

There is a way of thinking in the Kingdom of God. We have to be taught, to learn, to be trained to think this way. When a Kingdom mentality is understood, it will cause the kingdom of darkness to not prevail against us. The Kingdom must be placed above everything else and should have no competition. It must be our highest priority. In seeking first the Kingdom, the Kingdom of God must have first priority over any and every thing on this earth and in our lives. Our total and absolute allegiance is to be to God and His Kingdom.

There is a lack of responsibility in the world today from world leaders and world governments, including our own leaders here in America, from the office of the President to Congress, the US Supreme Court, judges, governors, mayors, law enforcement, corporations, businesses, and in society in general and ultimately the family. All these entities in some way or another refuse to be held accountable to anyone but are more willing to place the blame somewhere else. This in part, I believe, is happening because the Church has not fully accepted its responsibility in this world. Instead, we are waiting to see what God is going to do, but the answer is nothing! We must do something first and quit putting the responsibility and blame on Him.

The Kingdom Government of Heaven is only obligated to respond on earth when we give the invitation. Jesus said, "Whatever you ask of the Father in my name, He will give it to you" (John 16:23). I understand that the enormity of this kind of responsibility and accountability can be completely overwhelming. However, the Church must begin to take on this way of thinking, understanding that we are responsible for what happens on this earth. This is bigger than just you, your family, your church, your job, or your neighborhood.

Our responsibility on earth is far greater than we have chosen to believe that it is. Now I'm not suggesting for one moment that you and I are to take the blame for everything that goes wrong in this world to the point of condemnation. No! Nevertheless, individually and as the Church, we need to be willing to accept the blame and open our hearts and minds to the responsibility of such.

For this is the first step to repentance (changing the way you think) in order to receive the Kingdom of God. And the second step that will help in going from a worldly-mindset to a kingly-mindset and changing the way you think is understanding what the Church really is, and what it really is not.

Chapter 2

THE CHURCH—
A GOVERNING BODY

Our Legal Position

The Church is recognized in Scripture as not just the assembly, but the general assembly and Church of the firstborn, who are written in heaven (Heb. 12:23). This same word is used to describe a gathering of nations from around the world located in New York City called the U.N. or United Nations. It is from this location that decisions are made that govern world affairs. The phrase "general assembly" means the supreme governing body of some religious denominations, or entity. The U.S. Senate and the House of Representatives, which make up Congress, would be a general assembly, a governing body.

Jesus is the head of His spiritual body known as the Church. Just as the head cannot get around on its own, neither can the body know where to go on its own. Just as God in Christ by His own will has chosen to limit Himself in order that the Church may become His judicial equal, the Christ of God has made us joint heirs with Himself. This self-limitation of God by which I speak is prayer. Prayer is the vehicle in which God has made Himself dependent upon man. That's right, God by His own sovereign choice, in order that those whom He has redeemed, best known as the Church, may be able to exercise their dominion authority here on earth, has chosen to limit Himself.

God has become helpless in this sense. This is bad news for us because unless we pray, ask, invite, or speak His word in this earthly realm, He will remain on the outside looking in. This brings us back to the legal aspect of the word "judicial." Even though *Webster's New World Dictionary* defines this word as a delegated equality, it is as fully recognized and respected as if it were original.

This delegated equality is without a doubt implied in the term "joint heir" (Rom. 8:17). In legal terms, a joint heir can do nothing alone, nothing without the other. Jesus said, "Apart from me you can do nothing" (John 15:5), and without us He will do nothing: this is Christ and the Church. Our judicial equality is found in sayings such as, "If you abide in me, and my words abide in you, you shall ask what you will, and it shall be done unto you" (John 15:7). "Or, truly, truly I say unto you, he that believes on me, the works that I do shall he do also, and greater works than these shall he do because I go to the Father" (John 14:12).

"And *all* things, *whatever* you shall ask in prayer, believing, you shall receive" (Mark 11:24). How could we possibly do the same works that He did, and greater, if we did not have the same Spirit that He has, and the same judicial authority that He has? Because of the legal implications of this relationship between Christ and the church, God will do nothing apart from our cooperation; if we do not act, neither will the Holy Spirit. Rev. 22:17 says the "Spirit and the bride said, Come": not just the Spirit alone, but the bride also. But make no mistake about it, God is, and forever will be, the only ruling, reigning, self-sufficient, self-existing, almighty, eternal, supreme, and sovereign authority of all creation, seen and unseen.

Influenced by None— But Influencing All

The Church is a governing body, because the Greek word for "church" is not a religious word, but a governmental one. This would explain immediately why the church world does not think, believe, and operate the way that it should. Some say that it operates like a business: yes, like a business exactly. It should be genuine Kingdom of God business only, but instead it operates more like one that does not fully grasp its legal jurisdiction. We have allowed the world to define who and what we the Church are.

This word "church" was used by the Greeks to refer to political groups. The Church is the Greek word "*ecclesia*," or called-out ones, senate, assembly, powerhouse, or cabinet as in a Federal Republican form of government today. This senate was the powerhouse, the ones who are the closest to the King. Individuals who were personally chosen by the King or Emperor of that day received his instructions, directives, thoughts, will, desire, intent, and passion, and turned it into legislation that was to be implemented into the kingdom. This is really who and what the Church is: a governing entity, not a religious institution. We must begin to do now what we have been placed here to do, which is to exercise our dominion authority over all the earth.

As believers, we act as if the only influence that we have is in spiritual matters. We live in a physical world, therefore should we not also have influence on a physical level? Yes! Our authority may be in the spirit, but its influence is seen in the physical. Our influence should be in every aspect of society such as politics, government, music, education, journalism, science, business, finance, medicine, entertainment, and every other aspect and walk of life. We have the authority to change things in this physical world.

For you see you are a Kingdom-minded person, and a Kingdom-minded person never takes sides with an issue because of a person's gender, race, religion, faith, age, or economic status (rich, poor, or middle class), and never based on their political persuasion, be it Democrat, Republican, Independent, Liberal, Communist, Socialist, or Conservative. We that are in the Kingdom should bear upon this world the culture of the Kingdom of God, and not the other way around.

The Kingdom of God comes first. The decisions that we make as kings should always be based upon our Heavenly government's position, and if it is not, then none of the things that we look to implement from the word of God, or in this book, will be effective in our lives. We belong to a far greater government than the governments of this world, and we need to start living and conducting ourselves in this way. So when Jesus said, "Upon this rock I will build my church," He was not speaking of building a religious institution, but rather that He will build His governing body (Matt. 16:18).

For the Bible says, "And the government shall be upon His shoulder, and of the increase of His government and peace there shall be no end" (Is. 9:6). The He that it speaks of is Jesus, and the church embodies that government. This is why Jesus said the Kingdom of God (the government of heaven) is within you, because God's Kingdom government is in the Holy Spirit (Rom. 14:17).

God in Government

It is interesting to notice that the government of the United States is summed up in three words: life, liberty, and the pursuit of happiness. Just as God's Kingdom is summed up in three words: righteousness, peace, and joy. Authority and accountability are the two most important words when it comes to government. We are told in Isaiah that the government is upon His (Jesus') shoulder. Seeing that the shoulders of a person are on their body, therefore the church has been appointed by Christ to bear upon it His Kingdom government here on earth (Luke 22:29). It is upon the shoulders of the physical body that you can place the most weight. Notice those who work out in a gym: it is upon the shoulders that the individual places the heaviest of weights when it comes to doing leg squats. Clearly, everything is about government.

It was God who instituted government; it was and is His idea. If there appears to be a need for people in this world for government to take care of everything pertaining to their life, it can all be traced back to the first chapter of the book in Genesis which reveals the first form of government on earth, and that is a kingdom government in which God gave dominion to man (and woman). But the biggest difference is that it was not a government under the rule and authority of man, but under the rule and authority of the Spirit of God himself. It was this kingdom or government that Adam lost in the garden.

The purpose for government is to bring stability, order, protection, responsibility, accountability, and more. In other words, this involves people. Without people there is no need for government, and without government and law, you will have chaos.

It is this Kingdom government of heaven that man is looking for, because this is what Adam originally lost in the garden, and not a religion. Jesus said, "I came to seek and save that which was lost," but it is only through Christ Jesus that we can receive the free gift of righteousness and become a citizen of His Kingdom (Luke 19:10). This would explain why there are so many different kinds and forms of governments in the world today. Because apart from Christ, man is left to govern himself, and you see for yourself the turmoil: the spiritual, and social, and cultural conditions of our world that this self-governing has given us.

Religion, as the world has defined it, has caused

more confusion on the subject of God than any other thing. It has caused more problems, and given us more wars, mayhem, and mass murdering of the human population than anything else in history. Religion, as it is viewed by the world, is only based upon man's non-redemptive rituals and moral belief systems, which are always in disagreement with the word of God. Pure religion is found in James 1:27, and the Church, true Christianity is built by a King (Christ) and is functional by his Kingdom government.

Chapter 3

THE AUTHORITY TO GOVERN

I have a suggestion. The next time you come together for what we call a prayer meeting, instead of business as usual, where we usually make petitions, plead, beg, and even speak in faith, let's come together to seek the counsel of the Lord and get His instructions and guidance, His thoughts, will, and desire, and let's make a reality out of the words that invite His Kingdom to come and His will to be done on this earth, as it is in heaven.

Concerning God restoring our lives, families, jobs, new car, new house, or business or financial prosperity, all these things should be, but they have their place. Now more than ever it is time, through prayer, for the church to begin to set things right in this world.

True righteousness is found in God but is only available and obtainable in Christ. To be a righteous man therefore means to be in right standing or right relationship with God and with His way of doing things. But even for the mere fact of just doing what is right today, there seems to be a void, especially from those in authority. For it is righteousness that exalts a nation, but we must awake! Wake-up to what is right and sin not. Righteousness is always ready. Righteousness does not ask if you want to do what is right or not. It demands it.

We think we have been waiting on God. No! God has been waiting on us, and according to Rom. 8:18–22, so has all of creation, which says, *"For I reckon that the sufferings of this present time are not worthy to be compared with the glory which shall be revealed in us. For the earnest expectation of the creation is waiting for the manifestation of the sons of God. For the creation was made subject to vanity, (worthless; frustrated, empty of significance) not willingly but by reason of him who has subjected the same in hope. Because the creation itself also shall be delivered from the bondage of corruption into the glorious liberty of the children of God.*

For we know that the whole creation groans and travails in pain together until now. And not only they but ourselves also."

This is the most powerful yet the most humbling thought. Just imagine "all of creation" is depending on us. I told you before that our responsibility is enormous. Look at what happened to creation when man (Adam) lost his ability to govern it. The scripture says creation was made or became subject to vanity: it's frustrated, specifically because of the sin of man, but not willingly. People are frustrated, animals are frustrated, the earth itself, (the land) is frustrated. The sea, the environment, and the weather are also, and we ourselves are as well.

Frustration causes the opposite of what government was designed to do. It causes instability, lack of responsibility, disorder, no accountability, and self-governing. Some have the "I can do it myself attitude," as it relates to our own individual ability to live a moral life, or collectively as a people, and our government to manage our way of life. Let us take our position in Him from heaven to earth where we are seated with Him, and now let's use the keys of the Kingdom that He has given us.

Remember to bear in mind the purpose of keys. Keys are always associated with doors. Keys are a means of access, control, or possession. Possessing keys to something gives you access to something that you otherwise would not have or that others do not have. Keys give you control, which is one of the meanings of the word; to govern. Keys also give you freedom and responsibility. Jesus said, "Whatever you bind [lock] or loose [unlock] on earth" heaven would do the same, so whatever on earth is not "as it is in heaven," use your governing authority to make it right (Matt. 18:18).

Let's begin to allow only what heaven allows, and

prohibit what heaven prohibits, accept only what it accepts, and not accept what it does not accept. Yes! Start with yourself, then family, afterwards society, your community, city, state, nation, and the world, this is our responsibility. You have something to say about what goes on in this world. Now, I challenge you to make it personal, for you will then step into a whole new dimension and place of kingship in Christ.

It's Already Done

God independently and of His own sovereign will makes the decisions governing earthly affairs—the responsibility and authority to enforce and implement those decisions he has placed upon the shoulders of His body (Church). If it's allowed in heaven the church should allow it on earth. If it's not allowed in heaven the Church should not allow it on earth. Remember that the work is already done.

It was on the seventh day of creation that God rested from all his works. That simply means that He ceased from all His labor, because He was finished. And the church has yet to cease from its labor and to enter into God's rest (peace). What does that mean? Unlike governments who receive their authority by voting or by revolution, the church has inherent authority. This authority was given by the

King of heaven to kings on the earth (the Church), not earthly kings. Kings have the ability to speak and things will get done; they give commands and never have to try and make things happen.

We are those kings. The scripture says that He (Jesus) has made us kings and priests unto our God, and the power of a king is in his words. Eccl. 8:4 says, "Where the word of a king is there is power." When it comes to addressing the issues of our day, whether it is in society, in business, government, or life in general, our weapons are not carnal as are the world's. When we want something done we just believe what God has said about our authority and then we speak the results, and action is sure to follow.

This is that rest that God is talking about. For we who have believed do enter into rest, as He said, "As I have sworn in my wrath, they shall not enter my rest; although the works were finished from the foundation of the world. For He spoke in a certain place of the seventh day in this way and God did rest the seventh day from all His works. And in this place again, if they shall enter into my rest. Seeing, therefore it remains that some must enter into it and they to whom it was first preached entered not in because of unbelief" (Heb. 4:3–6).

The scripture teaches us that there are six things the Lord hates, and seven is an abomination unto him (Prov. 6:16–19). Yet the greatest sin of all is unbelief. Unbelief is an absolute insult to the Godhead. After all, this is God Almighty asking us to believe what He says. How does it make you feel when the people that you know and love won't believe you when you tell them something? Not to believe what someone says that you have developed a relationship with puts the relationship in question.

The sin of unbelief grieved the Holy Spirit of God for forty years by the children of Israel in the wilderness. In fact, God calls unbelief evil (Heb. 3:12). The writer of Hebrews is telling the story of what happened to the children of Israel when they believed, and when they did not believe. God was taking them to receive their inheritance, which was the promised land; it can only be entered into by faith. We have a promised land also. It is the Kingdom, our inheritance (Matt. 25:34). The scripture in Heb. 4:9–11 says, "There remains, therefore, a rest to the people of God. For he that has entered into his rest, he also hath ceased from his own works as God did from his."

Let us labor therefore to enter into that rest. There is a work that God is looking for, and it is called the work of faith. The inheritance that we have received from the Lord can only be accessed by our faith in what He has said. I must believe to enter into this rest. Self cannot produce this, my physical labor per se cannot produce this, striving and toil cannot access this inheritance. Instead, ceasing from the before-mentioned works as God did from His works, and laboring only in what He has said in His word, will cause us to enter into His rest or peace, and thereby start manifesting Kingdom results.

As it pertains to that which keeps us from entering into God's rest the word that truly stands out is toil. This word means to labor continually, physical exertion; exhausting labor or effort. The situation was such in the garden of Eden that whatever man needed was there, everything from his physical nourishment and food, to natural resources such as various stones and gems, to precious metals such as silver and gold, and the gold of that land the scripture said, was good. But after the fall of man he had to sweat, strive, and toil for what he needed, for he no longer possessed the kingdom, but this should no longer be the case for you and me today if we are in Christ. Even though God will bless the work of our hands, nevertheless, from the foundation of the world everything is already done.

Ruling From the Heavenly

By the blood He shed on the cross, He cried it is finished. Then after His death, burial, and before His resurrection, having spoiled principalities and powers, Jesus made a show of them openly triumphing over them in it (Col. 2:15). "Spoiled" means to strip the hide from an animal, to completely disarm a defeated foe, to damage, or injure in such a way as to make useless, to destroy.

"After Jesus was justified and made alive in the spirit, this is what He did to Satan. Afterward He arose from the dead and ascended on high and sat at God's right hand in the heavenly. Far above all principality, and power, and might, and dominion, and every name that is named, not only in this age, but also in that which is to come. And He hath put all things under His feet, and gave Him to be head over all to the church, (the called-out ones) which is His body, the fullness of Him that fills all in all" (Eph. 1:20–23).

For we can also see that God has made us alive together with Christ... "And hath raised us up together and made us sit together in the heavenly in Christ Jesus" (Eph. 2:6). Whenever the King's court is in session, or if there is a counsel meeting, those whom the King has chosen to implement His policies into the Kingdom are always there. This is exactly the picture and the role of the Church; as you see the Church seated with Christ, this is a picture of rest. You rest when you are finished with work. Now you may sit for a moment because you are tired, but even then the unfinished portion of the task is still on your mind, therefore you are not really at rest yet.

So rest is not just ceasing from physical exertion, but rather when the mind is at peace.

So when I pray I must pray from a position of being seated with Him. The fact we are seated with Christ in the heavenly puts us in a governing position here on the earth. We rule down here (on earth) as it is up there (in heaven). Not only is it true that one day we will rule and reign with Christ here on earth for a thousand years, and for all eternity afterwards, but the same is true even right now, because as He is, so are we in this world.

So how is He now? He is seated on the throne, so are we. He is far above all principalities and powers and might and dominion, and every name that is named, so are we. He is Lord, so are we. He is King, so are we. The Kingdom is His, as is ours. He has all authority and power, and we have been delegated authority and power. Now as I look at this from God's perspective, I can begin to see His intentions. Paul the Apostle, the author of the book of Ephesians, said that this intent was a mystery hidden in God that is now revealed unto his holy apostles and prophets, by the Spirit (Eph. 3:5). And that is unto the principalities and powers in heavenly places might be known by the church—the ecclesia, the powerhouse, the assembly, the senate, the cabinet, the manifold (or the multiple, many times, a great deal) wisdom of God.

We can see that the early church in the book of Acts operated very effectively in much of this, and so did many of the Old Testament patriarchs and the prophets. In Heb. 11:33–34 these Old Testament saints are the ones about whom it was said that through faith they subdued kingdoms, wrought righteousness, and obtained promises, and they did all these things with less available for them than what we have available for us in Christ Jesus. That is why I believe it is the Church of today that God wants to use to close out this dispensation with even greater glory.

We have allowed far too many things in this world and in society to go unchallenged, but not anymore! This is why people should be looking to the church and not the government, or the world, for answers. Because the Church is the best government agency on earth that can rightfully handle the needs of the people. Up to this time the kingdom of darkness for the most part has not been challenged, or put in check, by a far superior kingdom, the Kingdom of God. For it is the Church, not Satan, that wields the balance of power in human and world affairs.

Exposing the Problem

For we glory and rightfully so in Jesus who is enthroned in Heaven. What we have yet to grasp is that we have been enthroned with Him, and it is from that position that we must begin to operate in our dominion authority here on earth. There is much more resting that the church needs to do; we have tried far too many things in our own ability, and then called it the Lord's work.

We have even used the same weapons of warfare that the world uses in order to bring about righteousness and morality in society such as picketing, carry signs in protest, signing a petition, contacting the authorities, or any other thing that the world uses to bring about change. While at the same time we have been given by God the responsibility and authority to enforce His will and administer His decisions in the affairs of men.

The church is just as guilty as the world in putting its faith in politicians, judges, and lawmakers. Remember we are kings of the King, and as kings we have the authority to govern and legislate in the spirit, here on earth "as it is in heaven." Now doing some of these things such as signing petitions or protesting may have their place in some cases, and at a particular time. I believe even then, until our minds are at rest with what God has said about our authority, we will not be entering into His.

The Bible says that the weapons of our warfare are mighty through God to the pulling down of strongholds (2 Cor. 10:4–5). What are strongholds?

It is the Greek word "*ochuroma*," meaning fortress, a castle, a fortified place, words, thoughts, etc. that has fortified themselves in our thinking. The scripture goes on to say, "casting down imaginations and every high thing that exalts itself against the knowledge of God, bringing every thought into captivity to the obedience of Christ."

"Imaginations" is the Greek word "*logismos*," meaning reasoning, arguments, or logic. It is the way that people think based on their upbringing, life experiences, traditions, education, and so on. These strongholds are the mindsets of people. The term "mindset" is a combination of both "mind" and "set." It is the mind already settled on a set of beliefs, and therefore resists change. People are proud of the way they think, even to the point of being wrong: they would rather maintain their present way of thinking through arguments, debates, and reasonings.

These strongholds are also made up of demonic influence. Some believers have suggested that the way you pull down strongholds is by pulling down principalities over a territory. Well, there is no need to pull down that which you are above. You are not dealing with physically pulling down these demonic forces, but you are pulling down the fortress and the thoughts that are fortified in your thinking by the enemy. The scripture goes on and says, "Casting down imaginations and every high thing that has exalted itself against the knowledge of God." Two things are here: 1) it has exalted "itself"—it did not ask your permission; it didn't give you the chance to choose. 2) It has exalted itself against what God has said (His word), so as we govern in the Spirit, it will influence what happens in the physical, here on earth.

Chapter 4

THE INCREASE OF
HIS KINGDOM

"Unto us a child is born, unto us a son is given, and the government shall be upon His shoulder: and His name shall be called Wonderful, Counselor, The Mighty God, The Everlasting Father, and The Prince of Peace. Of the increase of His government and peace there shall be no end, upon the throne of David and upon His kingdom, to order it, and to establish it with justice and with righteousness from henceforth even forever. The Zeal of the LORD of hosts will perform this" (Is. 9:6–7).

This chapter and verse reveals to us that the increase of God's Kingdom or government will never end. It does not matter what the world says when it makes statements like, we are living in a post-Christian era, and that the Bible is an antiquated book that is not relevant for the present time. First of all the word of a king is law and final authority. As long as he is King the times in which He reigns does not diminish His dominion. And since God's reign and dominion is an everlasting dominion, that would make His word, the Bible, and Christians relevant not only at this present time but also in the ages to come.

Since there shall never be an end to God's government and peace, what should we the believers be doing? We should be busy being a part of the increase of that Kingdom.

I have learned to appreciate what Jesus said in Matt. 6:33, "Seek ye first the kingdom of God and His righteousness, and all these things will be added unto you": meaning that which is necessary for life that the Gentiles and the world seeks, will be added unto you. One of the most important characteristics of God is His righteousness. And it is His righteousness through Christ which we have received. In Ephesians 4:24 it says that we are to put on the new man which after God is created in righteousness and true holiness. Imagine that! A man (woman) can receive God's righteousness.

In order to get right with someone that you have wronged, you would need to meet whatever conditions that are necessary to restore that relationship. Therefore, in the case of God, you would have to be holy, perfect, sinless, and pure. Who among us in the human race can obtain that? "*No one can, for all have sinned and come short of the glory or righteousness of God*" (Rom. 3:23). Isaiah 45:13, speaking of Jesus, says "I have raised him up in righteousness."

Righteousness is the perfect holiness of God (Christ). It is an essential attribute to the character of God; it literally means one who is right. Isaiah 45:19 says, "I, the LORD, speak righteousness, I declare things that are right." Righteousness would be the polar opposite of sin, as to commit sin is to go against God and His way for our lives, therefore righteousness is the only standard that is acceptable for us to stand before the Father. There is no death in the pathway of righteousness, only life (Prov. 12:28).

A Kingdom of Righteousness

"For the kingdom of God is not food and drink, but righteousness, and peace, and joy in the Holy Ghost" (Rom. 14:17). Of all the things that God could have chosen to do in order to justify sinful man, He chose the only thing that was right for the job, and that is His righteousness. There is a lack of righteousness in the world today. I am specifically speaking of America and its leaders in government, businesses, churches, corporate America, and in society as a whole. There is a standard concerning what is right and God (Jesus) is that standard.

So how can one receive God's righteousness? Abraham was the first man to whom God imputed righteousness. To receive God's righteousness is not a mystery. Unlike religion, that tries to get man to produce His righteousness by what man does instead of by what he is, God causes man to become righteous from within so that his acts of righteousness will be because of who he is.

The righteousness of God is a very important key to the salvation of mankind. We should know this was true long before man was ever created, and even long before the Old Testament law was ever given: this was God's plan from the very outset. There was only one thing that God required man to do in order to receive this righteousness and one thing only—that is to believe, long before God ever gave the law to Moses for man to keep and live by, which was, and still is, impossible for man to keep. By nature man is a sinner; he is unrighteous. But it was through Jesus that it was said, "For he has made him, who knew no sin, to be sin for us, that we might be made the righteousness of God in him" (2 Cor. 5:21). And, "For if there had been a law given which could have given life, truly righteousness should have been by the law" (Gal. 3:21).

Only Believe

It has come to my attention, and now so many others, that in order to misunderstand God one would need an enormous amount of help in doing so, and God knows we've had a lot of help. It was God's desire to make it as simple as possible for man to receive eternal life. Man can never do or say enough of anything in order to be justified of his sins, because if man could actually do something himself in order to contribute to his salvation then he would have something to boast about. But God has already declared that no flesh shall boast in his presence.

"Even as Abraham believed God, and it was accounted to him for righteousness. And the scripture, foreseeing that God would justify the Gentiles [heathen] through faith, preached before the gospel [good news] unto Abraham, saying in you shall all nations be blessed" (Gal. 3:6, 8).

What those verses reveal is that it was always God's plan to restore man unto Himself, and that He would justify him through a faith that just simply believes what God has said. The way for a man to be restored back to God was never supposed to be complicated. God wanted to make sure that everyone had an equal opportunity to be restored. The word "inclusion" is a word that the world thinks it has cornered the market on, but according to this scripture in Galatians 3:8, God was the first to include everyone about this good news.

The covenant that God established with Abraham

happened 430 years before God ever gave the law to man, signifying that man would be redeemed by simply believing God in order to receive the free gift of righteousness and the promise of the Spirit through faith. No law was given (you do this and don't do that) when this promise was made. God gave man the law just so he would understand for himself that no matter how hard he tries he will never obtain righteousness by keeping the law. So, in time we will learn that the problem is not the law or something else, but it is what it has always been, us, because of the weakness of our flesh.

The world and religious man continue to struggle with this truth, and so do many within the church, that there has to be something else that I need to do in order to be made right with God. It just cannot be as simple as believing God's word in order to get right with Him or to receive anything from Him, but yes it's true, it is that simple.

Just remember it was in the Garden of Eden where not believing God became man's downfall. So is it no wonder now that believing God would be a requirement for man's redemption? Jesus did the very hard and difficult part by becoming our substitute. He did the part that we could not do; it was impossible for anyone to do what He did. By taking our sins upon Himself dying on the cross, being resurrected from the dead, and ascending into glory, seated at the right hand of God: all this was done on our behalf. Now, all we need to do is put faith in what God has done through the finished work of Christ and believe it. Because without faith it is impossible.

It is through righteousness that God increases His Kingdom: every time a heart receives Christ by faith, there the Kingdom has come, "For with the heart man believes unto righteousness and with his mouth confession is made unto salvation" (Rom. 10:9).

The Authority of Righteousness

I can recall many years ago one day out of nowhere fear came upon me. The Bible talks about not being afraid of sudden fear when it comes. Many times when fear comes for whatever reason, it is trying to convince you to receive it. The fear that day was all around me, because it was trying to get in, but this is the word that I heard on the inside of me: in righteousness you shall be established. I heard that two or three times, then I remember saying that's in the Bible. So when I found the place in scripture where it was written and began to speak it, the fear began to leave me as quickly as it came, because I invoked my righteousness in Christ.

Isaiah 54:14 says in righteousness shall you be

established; you shall be far from oppression; you shall not fear: and from terror; for it shall not come near you. It also says whosoever shall gather against you shall fall for your sake. Then it makes the statement that so many of us have learned, and that is: "No weapon that is formed against you shall prosper and every tongue that shall rise against you in judgment you shall condemn; this is the heritage of the servants of the LORD and their righteousness is from me saith the Lord."

Four things will happen when you are established in God's righteousness:

1) You shall be far from oppression and terror, and you shall not fear.

2) Whosoever gathers against you shall fall for your sake.

3) No weapon formed against you shall prosper.

4) You shall condemn every tongue that rises up against you, in judgment.

All these things will happen because God declares that your righteousness is from Him, says the Lord.

The prophet Isaiah in the Old Testament foresaw that it is through God's righteousness that man would be established in the Kingdom. This is why fear had to leave me that day as I began to invoke my righteousness because my authority in Christ is based upon that.

The Authority of God's Kingdom

Of all the things we have learned up to this point about God's Kingdom, it's a kingdom of righteousness (Heb. 1:5–13).

Vs. 5 "For unto which of the Angels said he at any time, Thou are my Son, this day have I begotten thee, and again, I will be to him a Father, and he shall be to me a Son, **vs. 6** And again, when he bringeth in the first-begotten into the world, he says, And let all the angels of God worship him. **vs. 7** and of the angels he says, who makes his angels spirits, and his ministers a flame of fire. **vs. 8** but unto the Son he says, Thy throne, O God is forever and ever; a scepter of righteousness is the scepter of thy kingdom. **vs. 9** Thou hast loved righteousness, and hated iniquity; therefore, God even thy God, has anointed thee with the oil of gladness above thy fellows. **Vs. 10** And, Thou Lord in the beginning has laid the foundation of the earth; and the heavens are the works of thy hands. **Vs. 11** They shall perish, but thou remain; and they all shall become old as doth a garment, **vs. 12** And as vesture shall thou fold them up, and they shall be changed; but Thou

Art the same, and thy years shall not fail. **Vs. 13** But to which of the angels said he had at any time, sit on my right hand, until I make thine enemies thy footstool."

So according to the scriptures, not only is God's Kingdom a kingdom of righteousness, but also a kingdom of authority. Did you know that this authority is because of righteousness? This is why God was so determined to impute to man His very own righteousness (the righteousness of God). Righteousness gives you and I Kingdom authority. We are always confessing and reminding each other that we have authority; well, this authority is rooted in righteousness.

The scripture says that the Father used the word again when referring to the Son as begotten, implying that He is His Son before His death and burial, and restating that He is His Son after He brings him back into the world through the resurrection. The Father says to the Son in Heb. 1:8–9, "Your throne O God is forever and ever; a scepter of righteousness is the scepter of your kingdom. You have loved righteousness and hated iniquity."

A scepter is a ceremonial staff or rod often used by kings. With its jewels and ornamentation, a scepter is a symbol of power (authority). "Scepter" is related to a Greek word that means to prop oneself or lean on something. That makes sense, since a scepter is something a ruler can lean on; i.e., royal authority, the dominion of a monarch (reign, sovereign). We can lean on God's righteousness; it is the basis of our authority. As I told you earlier, when fear came upon me suddenly, I began to invoke the righteousness of God, and the fear left me as quickly as it came. We have been made to have dominion in every way. If it were not for God's righteousness we would have no authority. Again, our authority is established in God's righteousness.

Can you remember the times when you have heard new believers, and probably yourself, after they have sinned, say, they think they have lost their salvation, and need to get saved again? Not so! It's not their salvation that they have lost; instead they have lost their awareness or consciousness of their righteousness in Christ. Their fellowship with God has been affected by sin; now the sin consciousness has taken over, and they are aware of the sin only. Therefore their faith is no longer operable, and they are not able to walk in authority. When you can't walk in authority you can't have victory over the enemy in any form.

This is when we should run to the Father quickly, not away from Him and hide in shame, but run to Him immediately. Do what He said in 1 John 1:9: "If we confess our sins he is faithful and just to forgive us our sins and to cleanse us from all unrighteousness." Once you are cleansed from that act of unrighteousness you become aware of your authority again. This is one of the biggest and most crippling tricks of the enemy, to get you into guilt and condemnation behind the sin you committed so that he can separate you from your authority you have over him.

Chapter 5

WHY WE WERE MADE

As you may have concluded by now, everything is about government. It is what God ordained to bring about law and order, and seeing that it was the Kingdom government that God first introduced to man, and the only one that has proven to bring perfect law and order, so it still is the only one that will bring it today. Man's greatest need and longing is to be governed by the Holy Spirit of God, whom he once knew: herein lies the great commission of the church, for it is in the hearts of men that this Kingdom must be established.

What is it to be governed by the Spirit? It is to come under the divine influence of the Holy Spirit, to be ruled, controlled, and guided by Him. Jesus was governed by the Spirit, for Luke 4:1 says that He was led by the Spirit into the wilderness. He also gave commandments through the Holy Spirit (Acts 1:2). Jesus himself said that when He the Spirit of truth comes He will guide you into all truth. The early church was governed by the Spirit also, for often the scripture says that the Spirit said this, or that, concerning them.

Every believer in Christ should be governed by the Holy Spirit, for Romans 8:14 says, "for as many as are led by the Spirit of God they are the sons of God." To be led or governed by the Spirit is not automatic; we must allow Him to do so. The degree that we are governed by the Holy Spirit is the degree that we will be able to govern in the earth. Everything is governed by something, and all things are governed by laws. Laws are fundamental principles that govern everything around us; they were created by God to serve His purposes.

Not just the laws of government, but also laws of every kind; such as the law of gravity, the law of aero-dynamics, or the law of sowing and reaping. There are both physical and spiritual laws, and in this case especially spiritual, because spiritual law supersedes physical law. The realization of this is found in these words: For the law of the Spirit of life in Christ Jesus hath made me free from the law of sin and death (Rom. 8:2), and since God is King of all that there is, or ever shall be, then that makes His word law and final authority, so in the final analysis everything is ultimately governed by words.

Everything that has happened, or can happen, will happen because of words. Words are not just abstract sounds, but as Jesus said, "the words that

I speak unto you are spirit and are life" (John 6:63). Words are spirit. Whether they are life or not is up to you and me; they can affect the spirit world, and they can shape and create in this physical world. Our words can be life, or our words can be death; after all, death and life is in the power of the tongue. Since it was a heavenly kingdom government that man lost in the garden, then it stands to reason that it is this same government that man is longing for now. We are, in these United States of America, a Constitutional republic, which is seen in a two-party government system. We are often confused about who and what to believe when an election is being held in our government; most believers aren't even sure where to stand on issues.

As an ambassador of a government by which you are sent to fully represent on this earth, you only and always have one place to stand, and that is for the policies that agree with your government's policies, the Kingdom of heaven. So don't tell me that my faith doesn't belong in government. My faith is established, and rooted in government. Our primary created purpose is to have dominion, and God would not have it any other way. One person is all it takes. There has never been a time when God has used more than one person to accomplish His will, and that one would then affect the many.

One person is all He is looking for. He is not

looking for a group, nor is He looking for a majority. He is God and He is King; He is a majority all by Himself, and that's why He only needs one person on earth to agree with His word. Now take that statement and make an even more profound point, and that is, there is only one man on the earth that can bring about the changes that we have been discussing, and that man is the head of whom we are the body, and that is Christ.

The Reason for Faith

Many believers are under the impression that faith is for just believing God for healing and blessings on our lives, our families, and our friends, and rightfully so. But it goes further than that. Faith is actually for influencing territory and advancing the Kingdom agenda. A territory is that which a king rules over, and without such territory (domain) the word "king" has little to no meaning. The word "kingdom" is from "king" and "domain." A kingdom is the "king's domain." The King reigns in this realm with complete sovereignty.

In Matt. 11:12 Jesus said, "From the days of John the Baptist until now, the Kingdom of Heaven is forcefully advancing and the violent [forceful men] take hold of it." It is high time to enforce Kingdom rule and authority here on the earth, by what we speak, declare and decree, and do. Jesus also said, "As you go preaching saying, the Kingdom of Heaven is here": this is a proclamation of invasion to the kingdom of darkness, not a competition but a takeover. This is also what the Lord meant when He said occupy until I return.

"To occupy" means several things, including to get and hold the attention of, to take over, to make busy, to move into by force, to seize possession of and maintain, and to take control over by or as if by conquest. This proclamation that the kingdom of heaven is here may not make sense to the person or people to whom you are sent to heal, cleanse, raise from the dead, or cast out demons when they hear it. But it is an announcement to the kingdom of darkness that a far superior Kingdom is here.

We have an entire perfect government system backing us up. There are so many things that we the Church have allowed to be occupied by the enemy, while we are left occupying very little, or worse, occupying the things that do not matter at all to the Kingdom of God. Satan and his kingdom are always operating in full panic mode, since the day of his annihilation by the Lord Jesus. Much of what we once held as true, sacred, and moral in this country, and in other parts of the world, have been seized by him. This panic mode that he is constantly in, stems from a fear that on any given day, at any moment, the ecclesia, the senate, general assembly, cabinet, the Body of Christ, the Church, you and I, and the sons of GOD will allow the manifestation of who Christ is in His glory to be seen in us by making our dominion authority a reality in the earth.

You are a king if you are in Christ. Where the word of a king is there is power, and because a king has absolute authority, his word is law. Yes, I realize that we have delegated authority, but within this scope of delegated authority from GOD, we have absolute authority. And know this: that our dominion authority has nothing to do with pride or superiority. It has everything to do with our submission to God's ultimate authority.

What Is Man?

Contrary to all the different reasons why some people say we were created, such as God needed us to worship Him, as if the angels innumerable as they are were not enough; or He needed us to praise Him, as if He has an ego problem; or that we were created to love Him or each other, and so on. Now all these are necessary, but only for us, not for God. "Need" is not a word that is acquainted with the Almighty. But there is a scripture that clearly defines why God made us: "What is man, that You are mindful of him? And the son of man that You visit him. For You have made him a little lower than the angels, and have crowned him with glory and honor. You made him to have dominion over the works of Your hands; You have put all things under his feet" (Ps. 8:4–6).

If you were to read this in the Hebrew language, the word "angel" is actually the word "*Elohim*" (English form, "God"): the first of the names of Deity is a plural noun in form, but is singular in meaning when it refers to the true God. The plural form of the word suggests the Trinity. So the suggestion is that He made man a little lower than (God) Himself. Remember earlier in this book we talked about how we, you and I, the church, have been raised up together with Christ and made to sit with Him in the heavenly realm.

There is no mention in the Bible of angels ever being seated, and especially seated with God. Only royalty gets to sit, the children of God. Kings sit on thrones, not angels; thrones are for rulers. We shall also one day judge the angels. God said that man is created in His image and likeness. "Image" here is from the Hebrew words "*tselem*" and "*demut*," meaning essential nature, copy, characteristic and essence. God is Spirit, and man is spirit. This denotes an expression of God's moral spiritual nature and attributes, making man "god-like" in this sense, as a spirit being. Some even teach that the temptation by Satan to Adam and Eve is that they would be God if they would eat of the tree of the knowledge of good and evil. Of course they couldn't any more become God than they could become Satan himself. No one can become something else other than what they already are.

Some even say that when we die and go to heaven we become angels. Even though angels have the ability to appear in human form, they are still angels, not humans. For you see Adam and Eve were already like God. The temptation would be that they would become like God, "knowing good and evil" (Gen. 3:22). It was the Jews who accused Jesus of blasphemy for this very thing. When Jesus said in John 10:30–35, "My Father and I are one," they took up stones to stone Him. Jesus said, "For which works you stone me, for I have shown you many." But they said, "For a good work we stone you not, but for blasphemy; and because that you, being a man make yourself God." That was probably the only thing that they ever really did get right during their encounter with Him, because He actually is God.

But it is what He said in response to them that we should be paying close attention to, because you know the Lord doesn't waste words. He said, "Is it not written in your law, I said you are gods." Notice that he said unto them, "I said that you are gods," and he was quoting Psalm 82:6. Further evidence of this is found in Exodus chapter 7, when Moses was told by God that He would make him a god unto Pharaoh.

Jesus continues in John chapter 10 and says, "If he called them gods, unto whom the word of God came, and the scripture cannot be broken…" Man was created god-like. This word "man" does not refer to gender, male or female, but to the spirit being that came out of God: spirits have no gender. Man is neither male nor female but pure spirit. If we refuse to accept what God has said about us, how can we fully become partakers of His divine nature? So let it be known that according to Psalm 8:6, we were made to have dominion over the works of His hands. It was this verse that God revealed to me that changed my life, though I had seen and read it much over the years. The way that I walk and talk, believe and speak His word has changed everything.

How to Have Dominion

We were made to have dominion. It is the will of God that I have dominion. The word "dominion" in the Hebrew is rendered, "*mashal*," "*mam la kah*," and "*malkuf*," and the Greek derivative is the word "*basileia*." The definition of the combined words is "sovereignty," "kingdom," "to rule," "to master," "to reign," "to govern," "to be King," and "royal rule," or royalty and kingly. Therefore, the word "dominion" means much more than just authority, and perhaps herein lies the reason we (the Church) fail to take full responsibility. The dominion authority for most of us seems to only be effective in the realm of demons and sickness, and even there we don't see the results we should.

I dare to say that according to the definition of the word dominion, our effectiveness in society and the world has fallen short. Therefore, another way of describing our dominion is to be established as a sovereign, kingly ruler, one responsible for reigning over and influencing territory. As I stated before, we act as if the only influence we have is in spiritual matters, but yet we live in a physical world, therefore should we not have influence on a physical level? Yes! Because our authority is in both realms, spiritual and physical.

I recall some 25 or 30 years ago understanding that I have authority over evil spirits and that I could cast them out. But most situations in life that you hear of or may have encountered does not require the casting out of an evil spirit, but rather it may require you to call the police, or some authority figure, for such things as violent acts, criminal activity, lawlessness, or corruption. Either way, we have dominion even over these things. And this is when my concerns ended, because many of these acts by others are simply in the realm of influence, and the sinful nature of man, and not possession by evil spirits. Nevertheless, my kingdom authority is in the spiritual and physical world.

When we govern in the spirit it influences what happens here on the earth, which is why we wrestle not against flesh and blood (people): we don't need to. But we wrestle against principalities, against powers, against the rulers of the darkness of this world, against spiritual wickedness in high places (Eph. 3:10). To wrestle with someone is to contend or struggle with an opponent as in close hand-to-hand combat, as by attempting to throw him.

It also means to strive in an effort to master something or to subdue it. This is why when a person is behaving in a manner that is contrary to the Kingdom of heaven, and you take dominion authority over that, your ability to govern in the spirit will cause that which we wrestle against to be overtaken and subdued. What are the works of God's hands? According to Psalm 102:25, the earth and the heavens (with all the natural resources of the earth at our disposal), and also in Job 34:19 it says, God does not regard the rich more than the poor! For they are all the work of His hands and so are angels (Ps. 148:2–6).

It is common in many Christian circles that we understand that we have authority over Satan, demons, sin, sickness, disease, and the flesh. But it has gone virtually undetected that we the Church truly hold the balance of power in human and world affairs. And that our dominion authority is not over just the above mentioned, but it includes the likes of lawlessness, corruption, violent acts, criminal activity, injustice, immorality, greed, and so on. The truth of this matter is found in Psalm 149:5–9: "Let the saints be joyful in glory; let them sing aloud upon their beds. Let the high praises of God be in their mouth, and a two-edged sword in their hand, to execute vengeance upon the nations [heathen], and punishment on the peoples; to bind their kings with chains, and their nobles with fetters of iron; to execute upon them the judgment written—This honor has all his saints. Praise ye the Lord."

Vengeance has nothing to do with getting back at someone. That would be revenge. Vengeance has to do with making things right again. Making things right for those that have been wronged, vengeance brings redemption and restoration. "Vengeance is mine says the LORD, I will repay" (Heb. 10:30).

But be careful that you are not among those against whom God is taking vengeance. Verse 9 above says that we all should be doing what verses 5–8 have declared. God has honored us with this, seeing that man is the work of God's hands, and that we have dominion over the works of His hands. That is not to say that man has dominion over man, no! God did not ordain such a thing.

We do not have control over each other, man over man (or woman), but we do have authority over that which influences or controls man. We have dominion authority over anything and everything that man does that is contrary to the Kingdom of heaven, or how else can it be brought to pass the saying, "Your Kingdom come, your will be done, on earth as it is in heaven" (Matt. 6:10). Remember what a kingdom is: it is the King's will over a domain, governing it by his will and influence.

Knowing that God made us to have dominion over the works of His hands takes believing to a whole new dimension. We were made and we are here to spiritually police this world, so to speak. We can neutralize a whole lot of things long before they ever even materialize, and we can put an end to many things that already have. Let's take a complete look at all that our dominion authority entails and its meaning:

Police—Maintaining order, to control, and to enforce the law.

Execute—To carry out fully, put completely into effect, to perform, to fulfill.

Let—To give permission, to allow.

Govern—To guide, rule, or control by right or authority; direct or strongly influence the behavior of.

Sovereign—Absolute authority, independent of, and unlimited by, any other.

Command—To exercise a dominating influence or govern authoritatively without question or opposition.

Manage—To control and direct, to treat with care.

Influence—The act, process, or power of producing an effect, without apparent exertion of tangible force or direct exercise of command.

Legislate—To make or enact laws, to cause, create, or bring about by legislation.

Decree—To determine or resolve legislatively, to establish a law.

Subdue—To conquer by force or by superior power and bring into subjection or order, to bring under control.

Law—All the rules requiring or prohibiting certain actions, a rule of conduct or action laid down by a governing authority.

Authority—Right to command and give final decision, delegated power over others, power to influence the outward behavior of others.

Judicial—a law or ordinance that is subject to enforcement by the courts. Decreed by or proceeding from a court of justice; "a judicial decision." Expressing careful judgment; "discriminative censure."

Enforce—To urge with energy, strengthen, constrain, compel or impose, implement, to effect or gain by force.

Dominion—Sovereign or supreme authority; the power of governing and controlling. That which is governed; territory over which authority is exercised.

Neutralize—when you neutralize something, you make it harmless, or ineffective, usually by applying its opposite force, such as pouring water on a fire. When we say something has been neutralized, that usually means that its power has been taken away from the outside.

Now, are you perhaps beginning to understand the depths to which God has gone to show forth the love that He has for man whom He created, for this is what He thinks about us, showing His opinion of us, by giving us dominion? Interestingly enough, in the New Testament the word "glory" is defined in the Greek as "*doxa*." I'll be the first to admit that I have done a lot of studying and teaching on the glory of God, but never once saw the word "opinion" as related to God's glory.

My pastor of the church which I attend made this known to us. This is a very important definition for us, because Isaiah 43:7 says that God created man for His glory. But this Old Testament Hebrew word glory translated here is "*kavod*," meaning weight, heaviness, honor, and majesty. The Greek word "*doxa*" has to do with someone's estimation or assessment. It is only used positively in the New Testament, so the estimation is always good and honorable. According to Thayer, *doxa* literally means what evokes good opinion, i.e., that something has inherent, intrinsic worth. In other words, God's opinion of us is summed up in all that has been revealed in this chapter, which is He has made us to have dominion over the works of His hands.

Chapter 6

A COMMANDING DOMINION

The true mark of a king is the ability to give command, but even better than that, it is to have that command fully executed. Instead of complaining and fearing and being at the mercy of situations and circumstances in life, we should not only have dominion on the earth, but God added one more thing to man's created purpose. He said to also subdue it, which is to bring into subjection or order, to bring under control (Gen. 1:28). Fear is never an option in God's Kingdom, and neither should it be in our lives.

God said in righteousness shall you be established; you shall be far from oppression; you shall not fear; and from terror; for it shall not come near you (Is. 54). Hence, we should seek first God's Kingdom and His righteousness because it is His righteousness that establishes us in the Kingdom. Once that happens, you (the righteous), become as bold as a lion. So do not fret the things that you hear and see, but rather be bold in the face of them.

"Why fret? Why cry out aloud? Is there no King in you?" (Mic. 4:9).

Many times we find ourselves crying out to God and asking Him to do something about the things that we are hearing and seeing, that are happening all around us. But the Lord's response is, the King is in you; you are as I am, therefore you do something about it. Kings should never feel inadequate or inferior in their own domain. So the real key to this dominion authority is this: acknowledging and settling this truth within yourself that you are a king, then the believing and faith comes naturally.

"Thus says the Lord, the Holy One of Israel, and his Maker: Ask of me things to come concerning my sons; and concerning the work of my hands, command you me" (Is. 45:11). Now this word from God has perhaps been one of the most difficult to receive and believe. I know it was for me, but once I embraced it, immediately it began to prove itself to me. I recall a series of events in my life where I began to command the work of His hands concerning what was happening at the time, and the results were according to as Jesus said, "The works that I do, shall you do also, and greater works than these shall you do, because I go to my Father" (Matt. 14:12). There is a commanding dominion.

God has invited us to command the work of His hands. God's rule of engagement is that heaven will only respond after we act first, which is to govern, execute, manage, legislate, judge, command, subdue, rule, control, allow, prohibit, enforce, master, police, and be authoritative in the earth. Upon trying to determine what would be an effective word to use for commanding, the Lord reminded me of the word that He used in the beginning to command.

And God said, Let there be light... and God said, Let there be a firmament... And God said, Let the waters bring forth abundantly... And God said, Let the earth bring forth the living creatures... And God said, Let Us make Man... And let them have dominion... (Gen. 1). Remember that to whom He is referring is the image of God, which is male and female combined, but is not two of the same kind. God uses the word "let" as a means of command, which means to allow or permit something to happen. For example, when something is happening around you, whether directly or in an indirect way, what is your response?

Do you say, "Well that's a shame," or the usual, "Well God's in control," or do you say "NO! that is not allowed to happen here, that is not allowed in the Kingdom, but rather let God's righteousness rule in this situation, or let there be peace in this situation," or let there be whatever is needed for the moment. You should say, "Father, concerning the work of Your hands I command this person, thing, or situation (that is contrary to the Kingdom of heaven) to stop now in Jesus name." I heard a preacher once say this: If something is not happening that you want to see happen, it's because you are not allowing it to happen.

It does not matter what it is that you are addressing, Jesus said, "If you shall ask anything in my name, [ANYTHING], I will do it" (John 14:14). With that kind of power made available, and in order to assure that I will receive anything that I ask in His name, the only thing I will ask then will be according to that which invites His Kingdom to come, and that which allows His will to be done. The Lord is not suggesting some far out, unattainable misuse of words when He says things like "anything," "whatever," or "whosoever." Instead, He is stating an unveiled reality of our dominion authority and what He would do based on what we can believe: therefore nothing is off limits, because God is able to do exceeding abundantly above all that we ask or think, according to the power that works in us (Eph. 3:20).

Praying vs. Saying

Prayer is a dialog between you and God. Prayer is that which is only addressed to a person. Since God is the only person to whom we are to pray, then if directed toward anything or anyone else, it would be idolatry. Prayer is a petition for God to act according to what we ask, based on what He has already said. Praying is always present tense. When we are praying we are in what I call the eternal present, where time becomes subject to you.

During prayer, suddenly you're not in a hurry: you don't need to eat, you're not as aware of your surroundings, you're not even so much aware of yourself, but you are definitely more in touch with God, and if you notice, some of these same things happen when you are caught up in talking about the Lord as well. That is because again you have made Him the center of attention. But there is one other element I want to explore, and that is saying.

Saying is synonymous with praying, except in this case the object of my words is not God, but it is the thing that my words are putting demands upon. There is praying and there is saying. Jesus said to the storm, "Peace, be still." Jesus said to the fig tree... Jesus said to the man with the withered hand... He said to the ten lepers... to the demon possessed.... "Whosoever shall say to the mountain" (tell it what to do) and so on, and then the Lord added this: "And all things, whatever you shall ask in prayer, believing, you shall receive (Matt. 21:22).

When Jesus fed the multitudes, He prayed first. Just a simple thank you to the Father was sufficient.

He also prayed before He commanded Lazarus from the grave, then raised him up by saying, "Come forth." Whatever things you desire, when you pray; believe that you receive and you shall have (Mark 11:24). Praying conditions you for saying. If things in your life, your home, your family, neighborhood, community, city, government, or wherever you may go on this earth, are not "As it is in heaven," then change it. You have something to say about what happens on this planet.

Asking is also prayer. This is why the Lord is opposed to those who pray using vain (meaningless, empty, useless) repetitions, because they think they shall be heard the longer they pray. But when you pray, He said, don't pray to be seen, whether in church or on the street corner. "Do not be like them," Jesus said, "for your Father knows what things you have need of before you ask Him. After this manner therefore, pray you: 'Our Father, who art in Heaven, Holy be Your name, Your Kingdom come, Your will be done on earth, as it is in Heaven" (Matt. 6:5–10).

Many of the founding fathers, the framers of the U.S. Constitution, confessed Christ as Savior and Lord, making them members of His body as you and I are. Without a doubt they were not faultless men; they were far from being perfect. Yet God in His wisdom used them to establish a government through freedom and responsibility that would allow the Kingdom to come and God's will to be done in the earth. How do we His body, the Church, fully regain what was once committed to our care? Let's begin here: instead of the Church being at the mercy of our elected and appointed officials through lobbying and elections in order to bring God's Kingdom and His will into the earth, let us not forget that we are a government within a government.

The Church is a Government (just not of this world) with all the rights and privileges bestowed upon such. Instead of being at the mercy and whims of our earthly government, we should be doing some governing, legislating, commanding, and executing of our own in the Spirit. This in turn can change the outcome of many of their decisions. This is why the scripture says, "You shall decree a thing and it shall be established unto you" (Job 22:28).

A "decree" is an act by someone with legislative and judicial authority to establish a law, or legislate. Once you make the decree, then begin to declare it, just like it says in Psalm 2:7. Make an announcement, and make it clear, so that the kingdom of darkness can hear that a king of the King has just spoken. In 1 Tim. 2:1–2 the word of God exhorts us, which is to urge, instruct, advise, or to make urgent appeal, that we not only pray for all men, and for all that are in authority, which usually includes God blessing them and giving them wisdom, but it also speaks of giving thanks, intercessions, and petitions.

Now concerning the word "petition," petitioning God is like exercising your constitutional right to petition the government. This is what you and I are urged to do; we are to petition God concerning those in authority as in petitioning the court for a specific judicial action: not just nice little prayers for them, but petitions for accountability and responsibility on their part also. Concerning the word "intercessions," we always think of this as being in a certain posture and praying, but no!

Intercession is the act of interceding (intervening or mediating) between two parties. It would be like you stepping in front of something on behalf of someone else which leads to intervention. This is what Moses did when God would have destroyed the children of Israel at one point, and this is what Jesus did for all of mankind when God would have destroyed us all, and yet He ever lives to make intercession for us. This is what we the Church must do for each other and for a world that is plunging deeper and deeper into darkness. Again, heaven is only obligated to intervene if and when we intervene.

- **Examples of governing in the spirit**: you would say: Let all those in government authority govern this nation according to the Spirit of God and the spirit of the U.S. Constitution upon which this nation was founded and the words it contains. I command accountability and responsibility from them the work of His hands. In Jesus' name.

I command the works of God's hand (man) all those in government authority, as well as those in society where there is corruption, lawlessness, greed, criminal activity, injustice, immorality, and violent acts to be exposed. Let the judgment written be executed upon them, vengeance on the nations (heathen), and punishments upon the people, and for these things to stop now—in the name of Jesus. Let the people to whom this government is of, for, and by rise up in righteousness; let them take hold of their authority until there is accountability, judgment, and righteousness. That is what you would call a judicial decree. *"Judicial decrees may not change the heart, but they can restrain the heartless"* (Dr. Martin Luther King, Jr. (1929–1968), American civil rights leader). My point exactly, well said.

But we know that judgment must first begin at the house of God (1 Pet. 4:17). And we also know that His judgments are perfect. Therefore let's embrace and welcome His judgments into His Assembly, the Church. And if at us first, what shall the end be of them that do not obey the gospel of God?

As It Is in Heaven

The degree to which we are to expect to see God's Kingdom come (manifest) and His will done here on earth is not as it is to my pleasing or yours, and not as it is in my local church, denomination, or religion, but always and only as it is in heaven. These five words are how we know when something is in line with God's Kingdom and His will. In other words, this is how God wants things on the earth to be, and therefore the goal of praying and the success thereof should find its results in this: "As it is in heaven."

The supreme sovereignty of God is seen in His willingness to give man dominion over the works of His hands, but not without the headship of Christ His Son. Ephesians chapter 1 says that when God raised Christ from the dead and set Him at His right hand He gave Him a name above every name, and that He has put all things under His feet, and gave Him to be the head over all things to the Church, which is His body. In heaven sits the Church in Christ, with Christ, because wherever the head is the body must be also.

The body of Jesus is a physical body, but the body of Christ is a spiritual body of which you and I are a member of if we belong to Him. If we are not a member of His body, then we do not belong to Him. The Church is His body, and the head cannot do what it wills alone, for the body has to do that. The body has no will, just desires, it can only do. Just as we use our bodies to do our will, so does the Lord use His body to do His will.

We the Church have the will of God in His word. Now let's go and do His will throughout the earth. For the Church is His body, the fullness of Him that fills all in all. For even the harvest of souls in the earth is dependent upon the church praying and asking the Lord to send forth laborers into His own harvest, and so are many other things dependent on the Church asking and doing. For example, we can clearly see God holding you and I responsible for what is happening, or not happening, on earth when He said, "How long will you [not God] judge unjustly, and accept [permit, allow, put up with] the person of the wicked? Defend the poor and father-less [orphans]; do justice to the afflicted and needy; and rid them out of the hand of the wicked (Ps. 82:2–4). Those who take advantage of this category of people, God calls them wicked.

There are wicked people and systems in place at this very moment to extort the poor and fatherless, and dangerously enough, one of the biggest systems of them all can be human government. For what was intended by God to help humanity can easily become catastrophic. The wicked can also be that individual who preys upon the poor, afflicted, widows, and the needy. You and I as the Church have been given the awesome responsibility to rescue them out of the hands of the wicked. We are told to defend and do what is right by them. Because when the wicked are called into account and are held responsible, they can no longer extort the poor and helpless. Wickedness exists because we allow it to; it's not up to God. How long will you accept the person of the wicked? Perhaps you are wondering, "If it's happening, isn't God allowing it? After all, He is sovereign." Yes, but we also know that according to 1 Tim. 2:4, it is the will of God that all men be saved.

But are all men being saved? No. God knowing what is going to happen before it occurs does not mean that He allowed it, nor necessarily makes Him responsible for stopping it. In fact, whenever God commands or instructs us about not doing something, He is indicating that He doesn't permit or allow it. Now let's look a little deeper: when a nation's government makes policies and passes laws that do not uphold even basic teachings in the word of God, then that nation is allowing its citizens to act contrary to the will of God and do all the evil that follows.

So you see we allow wickedness and evil to exist because of the motives of our hearts. After all, if we do nothing and say nothing about it, we are just being a reflection of those we choose to lead us. The powers that be are the ones who are responsible for such acts, and of course so are those who commit them. "WOE unto them who decree unrighteous decrees, and who write grievousness they have prescribed" (Is. 10:1).

This verse is also true spiritually concerning the believer who dares to decree unrighteous decrees also. Whether it is by executive power, legislation, or judicial decisions, the root cause for such irresponsibility can usually be found in Isaiah 1:21–23, but God also responded in verses 24–28. Furthermore the scripture says in Psalms 82:5–6—They know not, neither will they understand; they walk on in darkness; all the foundations of the earth are out of course (or the fundamental principles on which justice rest upon are all shaken) for this is the condition of this present world. But we have been commissioned by God to put it back on course again. This is God's way of seeing to it that things are done on earth as it is in heaven.

Prayers:

- Lord, as it is in heaven, let it be done here on earth.

- Lord, use me to govern in the affairs of Your Kingdom today.

- Father, let the governing impact of Your will, and your influence over a people and a government come! And what You want and desire, Your will be done on earth through my life today! As it is in heaven!

- Whatever I do today in my dominion capacity, let it be done "as it is in heaven."

- Govern my life today Holy Spirit: govern my heart, govern my mind, govern my thoughts, govern my will, and govern my actions.

- Father let the governing power of Your Holy Spirit rest upon me.

As it is in heaven: this is how we should be believing, praying, commanding, and expecting things to be here on earth.

Time to Possess the Kingdom

In the book of Daniel, Daniel sees a vision where he is beholding the excellency and the majesty of the glory of God (Dan. 7:9–14). He sees "The Ancient of Days," who is God the Father. Thousands upon thousands attended Him; ten thousand times ten thousand stood before Him. The court was seated and the books were opened (this is a scene of Satan's judgment): Satan's defeat was weighed in the court of heaven. Jesus came 500 years after Daniel saw this vision and explained Satan's defeat.

Jesus took away Satan's power and authority and destroyed him beyond repair. Furthermore, we also see one like a Son of Man coming with the clouds of Heaven. He approached the Ancient of Days and was led into His presence. This is a reference to Jesus, who also gave Himself the title "Son of Man" when He walked the earth. By virtue of His death, burial, and resurrection from the dead, He was given authority, glory, and sovereign power.

His dominion is an everlasting dominion that will not pass away, and His Kingdom is one that will never be destroyed, and all peoples, nations, and men of every language worshiped Him. But we also see in verse 15 that Daniel was grieved and troubled by what he saw, and he wanted to know the meaning of this vision and all the mystery that surrounded it. The one thing that was revealed to him out of the many is the one that has become so extremely important to us, and that is in verse 18 of chapter 7—"But the saints of the Most High shall take the Kingdom, and possess the Kingdom forever, even forever and ever."

And also verse 22, "Until the Ancient of Days came, and judgment was given to the saints of the Most High; and the time came that the saints possessed the Kingdom." That is from the time that Jesus regained it for us after Adam lost it until this present moment. Then verse 26–27 says, "But the judgment shall sit; and they shall take away his [speaking of the fourth beast in verse 23] dominion to consume and to destroy unto the end. And the Kingdom and dominion and the greatness of the Kingdom under the whole heaven, shall be given to the people of the saints of the Most High..." The Kingdom is ours to possess, but this is not automatic. The degree to which we will possess and enjoy it depends upon how much we are willing to be bold and claim what is rightfully ours.

A Kingdom may be defined as the sovereign rule of a King over a territory (domain) by his will, influence, and purpose. Without a doubt we the Church have been given more than we have taken full possession of. The Kingdom is ours; we have also been given judgment over that which does not reflect the Kingdom of God. Dominion is ours also; over anything and everything that is contrary to the Kingdom of heaven. It is the sovereignty, dominion authority, and greatness of this Kingdom that has been made available to us. "And this Gospel of the Kingdom shall be preached in all the world for a witness unto all nations; and then shall the end come" (Matt. 24:14).

It is the gospel of the Kingdom that the Lord has emphasized that we should be preaching, We have preached the gospel of Jesus, the gospel of salvation, the gospel of healing, of prosperity, of Christ, for all these messages are a part of the Kingdom, and we have accomplished much with those messages. But can you imagine what would happen and what the Holy Spirit could do if we actually preached the message that the Lord commanded us to preach? We would be getting the same kind of results that He did.

The scripture says in 1 Cor. 3:21–23, "All things are yours whether the world, life or death [because it is in the power of what you say] or things present, or things to come, all is yours." We own all things, therefore have access to everything. There is no Kingdom without a domain; a place to dominate (the earth). The kingdom rules over all!

To Sum It All Up

Once again, is God in charge and in control of this earth? He is in charge and control of His body like any head is. However, He is not in charge of the world system, though He is Lord of All! It doesn't mean He is not sovereign, but this is where you and I come in, the ones through whom He should and does control. It would be like you owning a house that you leased to someone else. You would be the landlord, because that's what a lord is, he is the owner. But the tenant, the one to whom you make the lease agreement with, would be the manager (caretaker). Both the owner and the tenant have control and are in charge, yet they are both limited by virtue of the contract agreement.

The owner can do anything to the house he chooses to do within reason, such as sell it, refinance it, or anything to do with the exterior or interior of the house or the land. It is the inside where the tenant will be able to exercise most of his or her authority, for both the owner and the tenant are sovereign in the matter. But regardless, whatever happens on that property, be it inside or outside, all that pertains to managing it is the tenant's responsibility, and the owner will gladly back him up all the way. Seeing this illustration was given to show you a picture of the sovereignty of God and the sovereignty of man (the believer), even though this is delegated sovereignty for man, yet within the scope of God's sovereignty, man has absolute sovereignty.

When you look at our form of government in America, you see three branches of power: Executive (the President), Legislative (Congress), and Judicial (the U.S. Supreme Court). The framers of the U.S. Constitution, the founding fathers, got the idea of a three-branch government from the scripture in Isaiah 33:22 that says, for the Lord is our judge, the Lord is our lawgiver, the Lord is our King, he will save us. We too, the church, the individual, have executive, legislative, and judicial authority. The big difference here though is that you and I do not need a majority in order for what we say to become law, because as kings we have been given this authority by the King of kings Himself.

When Jesus walked the earth, He demonstrated absolute dominion authority over all sicknesses and diseases, such as blindness, deafness, speechlessness, and the maimed; those without physical limbs, He grew them back. He took authority over all demons, evil spirits, and bringing the dead back to life. He ruled over weather systems and passed through crowds of people who intended to do Him harm, but they could not touch Him, and so much more. As kings, all of these things come under our dominion authority as well. With executive authority comes the power to execute; to carry out fully, to put completely into effect, and to perform our dominion authority.

In Isaiah 46:10–11 God said, "My counsel shall stand, and I will do all my pleasure. Calling a ravenous bird from the east, the man that executes my counsel from a far country, yea I have spoken it, I will bring it to pass, I have purposed it, and I will also do it." God is looking for the man that will execute His (word) counsel. Are you such a man or woman? This ravenous bird has characteristics like that of the office of an Apostle: an apostolic church (that's you and me) is one that executes to the fullest His word. It is time for the church to make policies like an executive that hell cannot handle. Through strategic spiritual warfare, with legislative authority, we have the power and responsibility to bring about change by legislation in the spirit.

Whenever we assemble together, Jesus said with just two or three, there He will be in the midst. Either way, since we are called the house of God, individually or collectively we become a house of representatives for the Kingdom of heaven. We are heaven's House of Representatives. With legislative authority we have the power and responsibility of enforcement of legislation that has become law, or that is the word of God and that which we have spoken that is in line with the Kingdom of God.

The word "judicial" also means a law or ordinance that is subject to enforcement by the courts, but a judicial act means an act involving the exercise of judicial power; one that determines controversies or questions of right or obligation. For we know that Jesus is the only true and living God, but as touching His manhood while He was on the earth, He also had judicial authority with the Father. He had a delegated equality. For He said, "The Father and I are one. When you have seen me you have seen the Father. I only do and say what the Father does and says" (John 10:30). For he thought it not robbery to be equal with God (Phil. 2:6), and concerning Christ, neither should the Church. By no means equal to Him concerning his Deity, but absolutely as a joint heir. The Bible says that faith works by love (Gal. 5:6).

Truly the missing ingredient to all that has been discussed in this book and all of this working is love. After all, God's Kingdom is a Kingdom of love. Is our love as great for the same world that God so loved? God's love was demonstrated in giving of His own Son. Jesus' love was demonstrated in giving of Himself, knowing that we were headed toward a collision with hell itself. He didn't consider His own well-being, but instead took on the full impact of that collision for us. It reminds me of a mother who seems to abandon all sense of reasoning and fear when her child is in imminent danger. To put herself between that child and the danger with no regard that her very own life may also be in danger.

This is the kind of love that the Church needs to have for the world that is in imminent danger.

When things in this world get out of order, it is our responsibility to see to it that order is restored. Here is an example of what to do. You say, "Let those in government authority, as well as those in society, who commit lawlessness, criminal activity, injustice, violent acts, corruption, greed, and immorality, let the judgment written be executed upon them, vengeance on the nations, (heathen) and punishments upon the people." This would be staying true to Psalm 149:5–9. The judgment written in the word of God is against unrighteousness, and there is a judgment written also by man in our laws that governs our society. This kind of commanding gives one a real sense of responsibility about where you are more likely to embrace the issues of life surrounding you, until you are moved to a point of action. For I long to see the day when the church in the twenty-first century would receive the same kind of respect that the early church had in the Book of Acts, and the children of Israel received when they left Egypt. Not only did God bring them out with silver and gold, and not one feeble among them, but Egypt was glad when they departed; for the fear of them fell upon them (Ps. 105:37–38). Lord let the fear of the church fall upon this world also. Let this be our legacy.

IF YOU'RE A FAN OF THIS BOOK, WILL YOU HELP ME SPREAD THE WORD?

There are several ways you can help me get the word out about the message of this book…

- Post a 5-Star review on Amazon.

- Write about the book on your Facebook, Twitter, Instagram, Linked*In*—any social media you regularly use!

- If you blog, consider referencing the book, or publishing an excerpt from the book with a link back to my website. You have my permission to do this as long as you provide proper credit and backlinks.

- Recommend the book to friends—word-of-mouth is still the most effective form of advertising.

- Purchase additional copies to give away as gifts.

The best way to connect or buy additional copies is by visiting www.kennethjcolemanministries.com

NEED A DYNAMIC SPEAKER FOR YOUR NEXT EVENT?

How about inspiring your group to the next level of success?

Without a doubt you were put on this earth for a purpose—and to the extent you live your life according to that divine purpose, you can expect to enjoy the fruitfulness and success that living "on purpose" can offer.

Hopefully reading this book has awakened within you a fresh hope and expectation that you were made for more and that your life, your company, your team can experience more in life.

But to get there often time takes some assistance. This is where I can help. Allow me to bring my teaching gift and leadership to work in helping you and perhaps others in your group to embrace a more full and faithful life.

To learn more about the specific talks and teaching sessions we have available, contact us by email at: info@kennethjcolemanministries.com.